Hapi

BY VIRGINIA LOH-HAGAN

Gods and goddesses were the main characters of myths. Myths are traditional stories from ancient cultures. Storytellers answered questions about the world by creating exciting explanations. People thought myths were true. Myths explained the unexplainable. They helped people make sense of human behavior and nature. Today, we use science to explain the world. But people still love myths. Myths may not be literally true. But they have meaning. They tell us something about our history and culture.

45th Parallel Press

Published in the United States of America by Cherry Lake Publishing
Ann Arbor, Michigan
www.cherrylakepublishing.com

Reading Adviser: Marla Conn, MS, Ed., Literacy specialist, Read-Ability, Inc.
Book Design: Jen Wahi

Photo Credits: ©Howard David Johnson, 2019, cover, 1, 19; ©Frontpage/Shutterstock, 5; ©Raimonds Romans raymoonds/Shutterstock, 6; ©Waj/Shutterstock, 9; ©Sergey Novikov/Dreamstime, 11; ©vkilikov/Shutterstock, 13; ©mario bonanno/Shutterstock, 14; Scan from The Complete Gods and Goddesses of Ancient Egypt/Wikimedia/Public domain, 17; ©S F-E-Cameron/Wikimedia/Creative Commons Attribution-Share Alike 3.0 Unported, 21; ©Ede Studio/ Shutterstock, 23; Leon Jean Joseph Dubois (1780–1846)/rawpixel/Public domain, 24; ©D.serra1/Shutterstock, 27; ©Mary Prentice/Shutterstock, 29

45th Parallel Press is an imprint of Cherry Lake Publishing.

Library of Congress Cataloging-in-Publication Data has been filed and is available at catalog.loc.gov

Printed in the United States of America
Corporate Graphics

ABOUT THE AUTHOR:

Dr. Virginia Loh-Hagan is an author, university professor, former classroom teacher, and curriculum designer. Like Hapi, she thinks a big belly is a sign of good health! She lives in San Diego with her very tall husband and very naughty dogs. To learn more about her, visit www.virginialoh.com.

TABLE OF CONTENTS

ABOUT THE AUTHOR 2

CHAPTER 1:
ARRIVAL OF HAPI 4

CHAPTER 2:
TWO GODS IN ONE 10

CHAPTER 3:
FAMILY SECRETS 16

CHAPTER 4:
THE OTHER HAPIS 22

CHAPTER 5:
LOST IN THE NILE 26

DID YOU KNOW? 30
CONSIDER THIS! 31
LEARN MORE 31
GLOSSARY 32
INDEX. 32

ARRIVAL OF HAPI

Who is Hapi? How is Hapi connected to the Nile River?

Hapi was an **ancient** Egyptian god. Ancient means old. Egypt is a country in the Middle East. It's in North Africa.

Ancient Egyptians honored Hapi. Hapi was an important water god. He was a god of the Nile River. He was the god of its **annual flooding**. Annual means happening every year. Flooding is an overflow of water.

Egypt is a dry area. It doesn't get much rain. But the Nile River gives the area lots of water. The flooding makes water spill onto the land. Water returns to the river. It leaves behind black **silt**. Silt is rich soil. This silt makes the land **fertile**. Fertile means capable of growing food.

The Nile River was very important to ancient Egyptians. It made them rich and powerful.

Hapi was celebrated with great parties.

Ancient Egyptians worshipped the Nile River. But they also feared it. A high flood destroyed cities. A low flood meant people couldn't grow food.

Hapi caused the Nile River's flooding. The flooding was called the "**arrival** of Hapi." Arrival means coming. A big flood was called a "large Hapi." A small flood was called a "small Hapi." Ancient Egyptians prayed to Hapi. They wanted to make him happy.

Hapi was known as a fertility god. He made the silt. He was called the Lord of the Fish. He was called the Lord of the

Family Tree

Parent: Nun (water of disorder)

Wife: Nekhbet (white bird goddess, protector of Upper Egypt) and Wadjet (cobra goddess, protector of Lower Egypt)

Child: Ra (Sun God)

Grandchildren: Shu (god of light and dry air) and Tefnut (goddess of wet air and rain)

Great-grandchildren: Geb (god of the earth) and Nut (goddess of the sky)

Great-great-grandchildren: Osiris (god of the afterlife and rebirth), Set (god of disorder and deserts), Nephthys (goddess of darkness and water), and Isis (goddess of marriage, fertility, motherhood, magic, and medicine)

Birds. He was known as the Lord of the River Bringing Plants. Because of silt, many animals and plants thrived around the Nile.

Hapi lived in a cave. He lived in the world's first waters. His home was the start of the Nile River. From there, the river flowed through the heavens. It flowed to the **underworld**. The underworld is the land of the dead. The Nile River rose out of the ground. It continued to flow through 2 mountains. The mountains were between 2 islands. The islands were Elephantine and Philae.

Hapi controlled the water flow. He brought the silt. But 3 gods helped him. Khnum, Anqet, and Satet left the right amount of silt.

Crocodile gods and frog goddesses also helped Hapi. They made the Nile River's waters cool and clear.

 Without Hapi, Egypt would have died. So, he was the most important god.

CHAPTER 2

TWO GODS IN ONE

What does Hapi look like? How is he like both a man and a woman? What are his symbols?

Some people thought Hapi was both man and woman. He was called the Father of Life. He was also called the Mother of All Men. He was responsible for all life. Ancient Egyptians loved the Nile River. The Nile was the center of their lives. This made Hapi very powerful.

Hapi had a man's body. But he had female breasts. His breasts fed the ancient Egyptians. They brought the rich silt. Hapi was shown as a big man. He had a big belly. This meant he had enough to eat. It showed that he was very rich and fertile. Hapi had blue and green skin. Blue and green are the colors of water.

Hapi wore a fake beard. The beard looked like a **pharaoh**'s beard. Pharaohs were ancient Egyptian rulers. Hapi's beard

 The Nile River's waters sometimes looked muddy and milky.

All in the Family

Nun was the oldest of the ancient Egyptian gods. His name means "primeval waters." Primeval means the earliest ages of history. Nun was the only living thing on earth before there was land. He lived in darkness. He was the water of disorder. From this water came all creation. At first, only frogs and snakes lived in this disorder. They swam in Nun's waters. Nun was called the Father of the Gods. He was dark. He was stormy. He was mysterious. He was boundless. Boundless means without limits.

He did whatever he wanted. He had no control. In some stories, Nun caused the Nile River's floods. Nun was a bearded man. Sometimes, he had a frog's head. He had blue and green skin. He wore large leaves from a palm tree. He didn't have any centers of worship. But there were sacred lakes and underground streams in his honor. Sacred means godly.

Hapi wore symbols on his headdress. Headdresses are fancy head coverings like crowns.

curled up. Pharaohs wore a straight beard. When they died, they wore Hapi's curled beard.

The Nile River had two parts. There was the Upper Nile. There was the Lower Nile. Hapi represented both parts. This is because the river flowed through both parts.

As the Upper Nile god, Hapi's symbol was **lotus** plants. Lotus plants are water lilies. They bloom during the day. They sink at night. They represented the sun and rebirth. Hapi's servants were crocodiles.

As the Lower Nile god, Hapi's symbol was the **papyrus**. Papyrus is a water **reed**. Reeds are tall grasses. Papyrus was very useful. It was used to make paper, shoes, baskets, rope, and boats. Hapi's servants were frogs.

Most times, Hapi was shown as one god. He was shown holding both lotus and papyrus plants. He held them in each of his hands. He was shown tying the 2 plants together. The knot means union. Hapi united the lower and upper parts of the Nile.

Papyrus and lotus plants grew around the Nile.

CHAPTER 3

FAMILY SECRETS

What are some stories about how Hapi was born? Who is Hapi's wife?

There are different stories about Hapi's birth. No one is really sure how he came to be. But a popular idea is that Hapi was a **creator god**. Creator gods made the world.

As a water god, Hapi was connected to Nun. Nun was the first waters. He was the water of **chaos**. Chaos means disorder. Hapi was thought to be part of those waters. At first, the world was crazy.

Out of these waters, a mound of dirt emerged. This mound was shaped like an egg. Sunlight hit the mound. It gave the dirt power. The dirt became Ra. Ra was the Sun God. As such, Hapi could be the father of Ra.

In most stories, Ra is the creator god. His father is Nun.

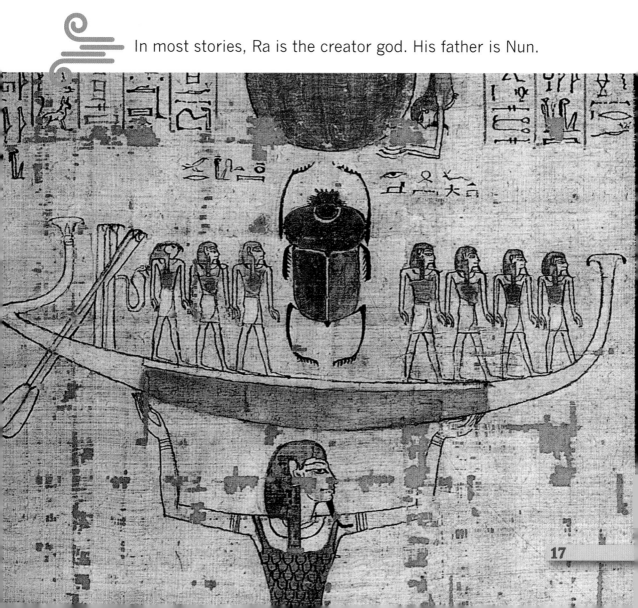

Ra spit into the Nile River. Hapi mixed with Ra's spit. This spit became Tefnut. Tefnut was the goddess of wet air and rain. She brought rain. Ra sneezed into the Nile River. Hapi mixed with Ra's snot. This sneeze became Shu. Shu was the god of light and dry air. He brought winds.

Ra and his family created the world. Ra made a perfect world. He cried tears of joy. His tears hit the earth. His tears became humans. His great-great-grandchild was Horus. Horus was the god of kings. He lived through the pharaohs. Through Ra, Hapi was thought to have created the world.

Hapi had 2 wives. When he was in Upper Egypt, he was married to Nekhbet. Nekhbet had the head of a white **vulture**. Vultures are birds of prey. They eat the meat of dead bodies.

 Ra and Hapi competed to be the most beloved god.

Real World Connection

Mostafa Habib helped start a project called Very Nile. He said, "It started as an idea 5 months ago when 4 of us were walking along the Nile in Cairo, which looked foul. And we wanted to help clean it up." Foul means dirty. The Nile River has a lot of pollution. Bad things are thrown into the water. Members of Very Nile host monthly cleanup events. At one of their events, over 250 people showed up. They came on boats and ships. They removed 1.5 tons of garbage. They mostly removed plastic. Very Nile wants to do more than big events. It wants to make a change every day. So, the group works with fishermen. Fishermen work on the river every day. They make a living from the Nile. Very Nile asks fishermen to gather plastic. They give fishermen money for the plastic. They recycle or reuse the plastic.

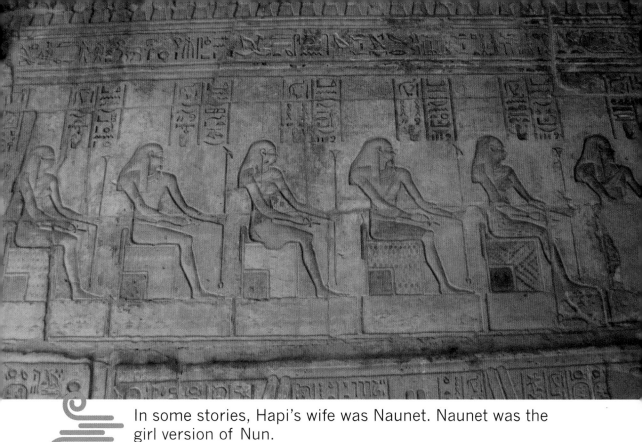

In some stories, Hapi's wife was Naunet. Naunet was the girl version of Nun.

When Hapi was in Lower Egypt, he was married to Wadjet. Wadjet had a cobra's head. Cobras are deadly snakes. They have hoods. They have fangs.

Together, Nekhbet and Wadjet were called the Two Ladies. Both goddesses protected their cities. They protected the pharaohs. They protected nature. They helped women give birth. They took care of babies left around the Nile River.

CHAPTER 4

THE OTHER HAPIS

Who are the other characters known as Hapi? How is Hapi connected to them?

The ancient Egyptians used Hapi's name in other stories. Hapi was confused for other gods.

Horus was the god of kings. He had 4 sons. His sons watched entire world. Hapi was one of his sons. He guarded the north. He was a **baboon**. Baboons are monkeys.

Ancient Egyptians turned dead bodies into **mummies**. Mummies are wrapped bodies. People's organs were taken out. These organs were saved in special jars. Horus's 4 sons protected the organs. Hapi protected the lungs. Some people died in the Nile. Water filled their lungs. People stopped breathing. They died.

Horus's sons were called the Sons of Horus.

Hapi the bull was also called Apis.

There's another Hapi. This Hapi had a bull's head. Sometimes, he was a bull. He was worshipped in Memphis, Egypt. He wore a sun **disc** between his horns. Discs are flat circles. Hapi was black and white. He had special markings. These markings were made from a ray of light from heaven. Hapi had a triangle on his forehead.

Hapi was also a fertility god. He helped grow grain. He kept **herds** of animals healthy. Herds are groups. Hapi kept life in balance. He represented power. There was an event called the Running of Hapi. This was done to fertilize the land.

Cross-Cultural Connection

Gonggong was a Chinese water god. He was the god of floods. He had a man's face. He had red hair. He had a black dragon's tail. He had a pet dragon named Xiangyao. His dragon had 9 heads. Gonggong was evil. He caused floods. In one story, Gonggong fought the Chinese god of fire. He wanted the throne of heaven. He lost. He got mad. He hit his head against a mountain. This mountain was holding up the sky. As such, Gonggong knocked Earth off its orbit. This caused Earth to tilt. This is why the rivers of China flow to the southeast. This also caused great floods. A goddess cut off the legs of a giant turtle. She used these legs to hold up the sky. This ended the floods.

CHAPTER 5

LOST IN THE NILE

What is a popular story about the Nile River? How does Hapi help Isis?

Isis and Osiris were powerful gods. They got married. They ruled the world. Set was the god of chaos and disorder. He was jealous. He wanted power. He tricked Osiris. He made Osiris get into a **coffin**. Coffins are cases that hold dead bodies. He threw the coffin into the Nile River.

Hapi floated Osiris to the sea. Isis was sad. She searched for Osiris. She cried and cried. She flooded the river with her tears. So, Hapi helped Isis. Isis found the coffin with Osiris. Hapi brought him back to life.

Set found out. He hacked Osiris's body into many pieces. He scattered his body parts all over. He threw some parts in the Nile. A fish ate those parts of Osiris. Ancient Egyptians believed those parts made the Nile River more powerful.

Isis put Osiris back together. Osiris lived and died. His life was like the coming and going of water.

The ancient Egyptian gods married their own family members. They did this to keep royal blood in the family.

Explained By Science

The Nile River spreads out and drains into the Mediterranean Sea. This area forms a triangle. This triangle is called the Nile Delta. The Nile Delta is one of the world's largest river deltas. It's about 100 miles (161 kilometers) long from north to south. It spreads out along about 150 miles (241 km) of Egyptian coasts. Deltas form when silt collects at the mouths of large rivers. They're rich areas for growing and life. It's very fertile. People have farmed it for thousands of years. Ancient Egyptians called the river Aur. Aur means "black." Silt is black. The flowing of rivers picks up rocks and minerals. It grinds them down into fine bits. These bits become silt. Silt settles in still water. It's rich soil. It's good for growing. It holds in water for plants.

In some stories, Isis is thought to be Hapi's wife.

Isis had a son. Her son was Horus. She needed to protect him from Set. She hid him by the Nile River. Hapi helped protect him. Horus fought Set when he was older. Horus took back Osiris's throne. Horus lived through all the pharaohs.

Hapi and Isis worked together. Hapi brought the floods. Isis taught people how to farm the land.

Don't anger the gods. Hapi had great powers. And he knew how to use them.

DID YOU KNOW?

- Hapi was also spelled Hep, Hap, and Hapy.

- Many songs were written for Hapi. But he didn't have any temples. Temples are like churches. They're places of worship.

- The Aswan Dam was finished in 1971. Dams block water. This dam controlled the flooding of the Nile River. Aswan is a city in southern Egypt. Gebel el-Silsila is a city north of Aswan. Both cities are close to the Nile River. People from these areas worshipped Hapi. They gave him gifts. They threw these gifts into the river.

- Akhenaten was a pharaoh. He ruled for 17 years. He died around 1336 BCE. He's famous for stopping the worshipping of many gods. He only believed in one god, Aten. Aten was the Sun God. But Akhenaten couldn't stop people from worshipping Hapi. Belief in Hapi was too strong. So, Akhenaten said he was the human form of Hapi.

- An amphora is a tall jar. It has 2 handles. It has a narrow neck. Hapi was often shown pouring water from an amphora.

- Sometimes, Hapi was shown as a blue hippo with broken legs. Hippos are dangerous water animals. They attack. So, people broke the hippo's legs. This was to protect the dead in the afterlife.

- In some stories, Hapi was an evil power. He worked for the pharaoh.

- The Nile River is over 4,000 miles (6,437 km) long. It's the world's longest river. It runs through Kenya, Eritrea, Congo, Burundi, Uganda, Tanzania, Rwanda, Egypt, Sudan, and Ethiopia. Most of ancient Egypt's cities are located along the Nile River.

CONSIDER THIS!

TAKE A POSITION! There are often different versions of the same story. In some stories, Ra created the world. In other stories, Hapi created the world. Which story do you like best? Why? Argue your point with reasons and evidence.

SAY WHAT? Read the 45th Parallel Press book about Isis. How are Hapi and Isis connected? Explain how they're alike. Explain how they're different.

THINK ABOUT IT! Learn more about the Nile River. This river was the reason for the success of the ancient Egyptian world. Why is water so important for cities and people?

LEARN MORE

Braun, Eric. *Egyptian Myths*. North Mankato, MN: Capstone Press, 2019.

Napoli, Donna Jo, and Christina Balit (illust.). *Treasury of Egyptian Mythology: Classic Stories of Gods, Goddesses, Monsters, and Mortals*. Washington, DC: National Geographic Kids, 2013.

Reinhart, Matthew, and Robert Sabuda. *Gods and Heroes*. Somerville, MA: Candlewick Press, 2010.

GLOSSARY

ancient (AYN-shuhnt) old, from a time long ago

annual (AN-yoo-uhl) happening every year

arrival (uh-RYE-vuhl) the coming of something

baboon (bah-BOON) world's largest monkey

chaos (KAY-ahs) disorder

coffin (KAW-fin) a case that holds a dead body

creator god (kree-AY-tur GAHD) a god who made the world

disc (DISK) flat circle

fertile (FUR-tuhl) having the ability to grow more crops or make more babies

flooding (FLUHD-ing) an event in which water spills over onto banks

herds (HURDZ) groups

lotus (LOH-tuhs) water lily

mummies (MUHM-eez) wrapped bodies as a part of the process of preserving bodies over time

papyrus (puh-PYE-ruhs) water reed used to make many things

pharaoh (FAIR-oh) an ancient Egyptian ruler

reed (REED) tall grass

silt (SILT) rich, fertile soil that is good for growing crops

underworld (UHN-dur-wurld) the land of the dead

vulture (VUHL-chur) a bird of prey that eats the meat of dead bodies

INDEX

E
Egypt, 4

H
Hapi, 30
  birth of, 16–18
  family, 7, 17–18
  how he helped Isis, 26–27, 29
  stories about, 22–25
  symbols, 15
  what he looked like, 10–11, 13, 24
  who he is, 4–9
  wives, 7, 18, 21, 29
Horus, 18, 22–23, 29

I
Isis, 7, 26–29

N
Nile River, 4–5, 6, 8, 10–15, 18, 20, 21, 23, 26–30
Nun, 7, 12, 16, 17, 21

O
Osiris, 7, 26–28, 29

R
Ra, 7, 17–18

S
Set, 7, 26–27, 29
Shu, 7, 18
silt, 5, 7, 8, 10, 28

T
Tefnut, 7, 18

U
underworld, 8